Do one small thing today to take you to realize your dream.

- Problogger Founder, Darren Rowse

Quit Your Day Job! Five steps to turn your passion to money using blogging and social media.

Printed in the United States

ISBN-13: 978-1515300731

© 2015 by Bukola Oriola

Revised 2017

Bukola Publishing (Bukola Braiding & Beauty Supply)

1628 County Highway 10 #210

Spring Lake Park MN 55432

763-516-4359

Email: info@bukolabraiding.com

Quit Your Day Job!

Five steps to turn your passion to money using blogging and social media.

By Bukola Oriola

Contents

Quit Your Day Job! 5

   Five steps to turn your passion to money using blogging and social media 5

Choose a name 7

Open a Gmail Account 8

Create a Blogger Account & Begin to Write 11

   Writing Your Blog Posts 16

Set Up Social Media Pages 18

   Facebook: 19

   Google Plus 20

   YouTube: 20

   Periscope 21

Google AdSense 22

   Direct Advertisement and sponsored posts: 25

   Monitoring your blog site for performance 28

   Google Analytics 28

   Bonus 30

References & Resources 35

Quit Your Day Job!

Five steps to turn your passion to money using blogging and social media

First, I want you to understand that the suggestions that I have made in this book is not a get rich quick scheme. It is a plan that you can use to build your passion into a profitable career through blogging or what some other people may refer to as content publishing or passive income. If you put the work in, it will give you a sustainable income.

It is not cheap. It is not easy. It takes hard work and consistency. Sometimes, you may even try various options before you find your sweet spot. By saying your sweet spot, I mean the topic or article that will bring you the following (fans) or engaged audience, attract advertisers, and make the money that you desire.

In the beginning, your goal should be getting your message out in a clear and concise manner. Online readers are impatient. They skim through stories to find the juice or "gold" that is in it for them. Therefore, you have to learn how to break up your articles such that a reader can quickly find what he or she needs in your story.

On the other hand, you can write short stories and refer your readers to other articles that are relevant, or that will provide the depth for them. If you decided to publish long articles, break them up into sub heads or even series or parts to make it less overwhelming for the reader.

NOTE: If you already have a website for your blog or business, jump right to "Set up Social Media pages." And, if you already have both set up, jump right to Google AdSense (check to see if Google Adsense is available to your country or the country where your site is hosted). However, I will ask you to back up a little to "Writing Your Blog Posts" and take a look at the blogging calendar. It will be of great value to you.

You have to also be careful of plagiarism when writing for the online users. Make sure that you cite your sources. Citing your sources will make you an expert and credible writer. If you hire freelancers or welcome guest posts, you can check for plagiarism at http://smallseotools.com/plagiarism-checker/. The website will let you check for plagiarism free of charge with up 1000 words.

Now that we got the few basic introductions out of the way, I will provide five simple steps you can take to get you started with $0. As you grow, remember that you will need to start spending money, perhaps, for advertisement to promote your blog in order to gain traffic that will culminate in buyers, or will result in getting you advertisements on your website or blog site.

Another interesting fact about blogging is, if you have a lot or articles about a specific subject, let's say, fashion or photography, for example, you can turn it into an e-book to sell on amazon and your website. You can turn any topic blogs to an e-book. The options are limitless.

I will write these five points in the order that you should implement them.

1. Choose a name
2. Open a new Gmail account

3. Create a blogger account (its available through Gmail) & Choose your story idea or ideas (start writing immediately)
4. Set up social media platform
5. Add Google AdSense to your blog

After reading the five points, you must be thinking, this is super easy! Yes, it is super easy when you know what to do.

I will like to caution you, however, that there is a learning curve. One of the things you want to do is to learn from other bloggers…. Read, read, and read. Sign up for *Google Alerts* at https://www.google.com/alerts on topics that you are interested in to get other posts or writings that will give you ideas. For example, I write about human trafficking issues, so I signed up to receive *Google Alerts* on human trafficking. I also write about business as I am doing in this book. I added business tips to my *Google Alerts*. *Google Alerts* is delivered to your inbox daily.

Choose a name

Choosing a name for your blog can be both easy and daunting at the same time. The easiest way to go is to just use your own name if you don't know what name to choose for your blog. Depending on your area of focus, you can choose a name that immediately tells your visitors what your blog is about. For example, I started a blog site focusing on weddings. I named it Weddings Trends. That tells readers that the blog site is about wedding related information. You can check it out through this link http://www.weddingstrends.com/. I hired writers to contribute articles on the side to keep it running since I am very busy with other businesses and advocacy.

And if you decide to use your own name, the visitors will immediately identify your ownership of the blog site. A blog site I started with my name is *All Things Bukola Oriola*. I actually changed the name of a *BlogSpot* I had to this new name. I have several websites focusing on various topics from hair braiding to human trafficking. I decided to use the *BlogSpot* to keep everything in one place. That is, I created links from the *BlogSpot* to the various websites. You can check *All Things Bukola Oriola* out through this link http://allthingsbukolaoriola.blogspot.com/.

There are sites that are started with the person's name. One example is the *Linda Ikeji's Blog*. She just used her name to start and she covers various topics and gossips. You can check out her blog through this link http://lindaikeji.blogspot.com/.

I hope these examples have given you an idea of how to choose a name for your blog site.

Open a Gmail Account

I recommend opening a brand new Gmail account for your blog site because it will afford you the opportunity to start with a lot of space. Google assigns 15 gigabytes to every email account. Starting with a brand new Gmail Account will give you that much space to work with. More so, you will be able to use the name of your BlogSpot as your email address. That way, if you don't want to share your personal email address with the whole world, you can keep your it from the whole world.

Another important thing about that is the idea of starting your blog on a clean slate. If the name you have chosen is not available on Gmail, use any of the recommended names given by Gmail or add your own letters or numbers to it to open your account. For example, when we wanted to set up the Gmail account and blogger site for a site with two friends, *Career Guide*, we added the initials of our names both for the website's URL and the email address because *career guide* was not available. But the name of the *BlogSpot* is *Career Guide*.

Keep in mind that your blog will grow as you work consistently on it, so make it easier for your readers, and buyers (sponsors, advertisers, etc.) to reach you with an email that is not too hard to make mistake on while trying to reach you by email.

Once you open your Gmail account, go over to the box that looks like little boxes on the right hand corner at the top. Click on the icon beside your account name. See illustration below.

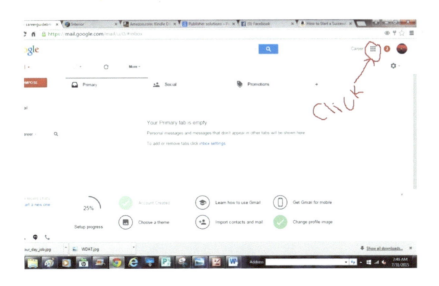

When you click on the icon, a pop up box will open showing various other applications of Google. Click on more. See image illustration below.

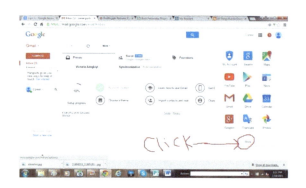

Once you click on "more" you will be able to see other applications, including the **Blogger**, the actual application you are looking for. Click on *Blogger*. See illustration below.

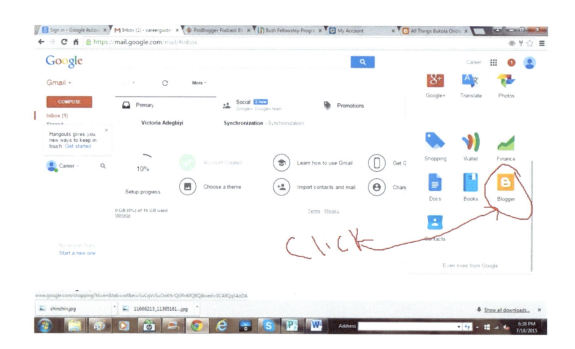

Create a Blogger Account & Begin to Write

It is time to create your *Blogger* Account and begin to write immediately. Once you click on *Blogger*, a new page will show up. Click on "New Blog" as shown in the illustration below. After clicking on "New Blog," a pop up box will appear on the screen. In the title box, you will write the name of your blog (the name you have chosen). Write the name of the blog in the address box. Mind you, it can be tricky. Your name might not be available for an address. Remember, if you had this issue when you were creating your new Gmail account, you might have it in this session. But do not fret. Just use the Gmail address as

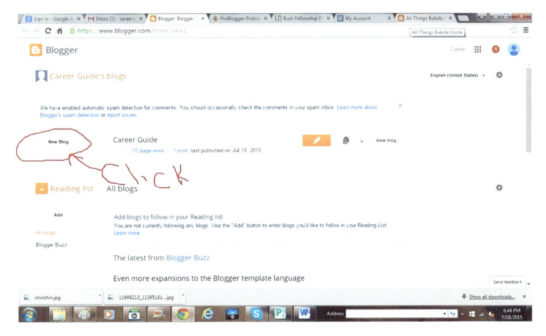

your address. Note that, the address in your Gmail must match or almost match your blog name to help users find you online and to give your followers the confidence that they are reaching you whenever they are trying to contact you by email.

Another thing to take note of at this point is the template. There used to be six designed templates to choose from – *Simple, Dynamic Views, Picture Windows, Awesome Inc., Watermark*, and *Ethereal*. Now, Blogger has added some new templates that you can also choose from. You can choose any one you like. See illustration below. For the purpose of this book, I will choose "Simple Template." Note also that you can always modify this template without using Hyper Text Markup Language (HTML) code. Click "Create blog!" See illustration below.

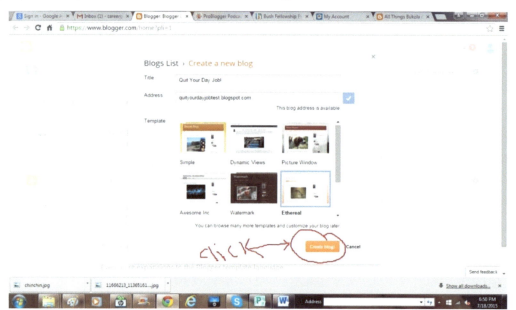

Once you click on *Create Blog*, a pop up box will appear trying to sell a domain name to you. If you want, you can go for it. It's only $12 per year. I have some Blogger websites with custom domain names. Weddings Trends is one of such websites. If Google custom domain is not available in your country, as this is new and not available in every country around the world yet, you can try a third-party domain and connect it with your blogger website. I use Blue Host for my domain names on other websites outside of BlogSpot.

You can ignore the advertisement by clicking "No thanks." See illustration below. You can still buy the Google custom domain or a third-party domain after setting up your site, or you can skip it all together if the Google custom domain is not available in your country. Your Blog site will still work just fine.

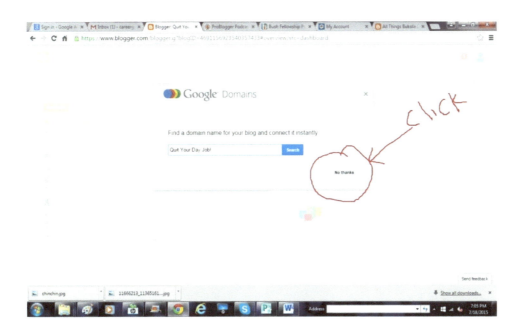

You will be brought to the overview page of your *BlogSpot*. At the overview page, familiarize yourself with the various links on the left hand side of the page. The items are right below Posts. You will also notice that the "book" icon. You will see "View Blog" right above that and the name of your blog on top of "View Blog". When you click on another item under "Posts", that item will change color to orange. Other items under "Posts" are Stats, Earnings, Campaigns, *Pages, Layout, Theme, and Settings.*

You can choose to create a new post right away or choose to design your template. See illustration below. You design your template under "Layout." Basically, what this means is that you choose color, the side bar, footer, and so on when you click on the "design" tab. You can also choose to leave it as the default design that is already available. If you choose the default design, all you need to do at this point is to start writing, that is, New Post.

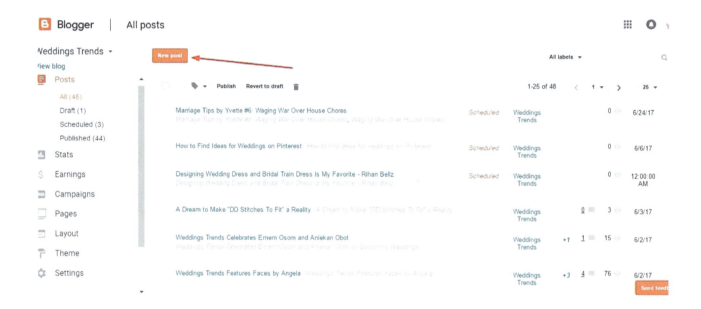

Take your time to study the various tabs. Play around and don't worry about making mistakes. It is in the process of making mistakes that you will learn a lot by yourself.

Note: There is a big difference between **New Post** and **New blog**. Proceed with caution! If you choose "New blog" from the drop down menu on your blog name, you will be creating a brand new blog. Google Blogger allows you to create up to 100 blogs. So, you can see that the sky is your limit. You can choose to have various topics as independent *BlogSpots*. But you need to understand that if you are writing a post for a particular blog, you need to choose "New Post." See screenshot below.

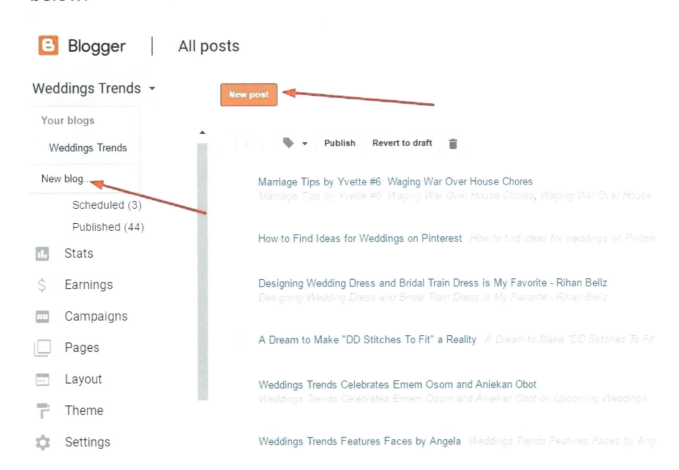

Writing Your Blog Posts

Now that you have created your *Blogger* account, the next step is to start filling it up with content. You choose what you want to write about. You can write about anything from hobby to politics. For example, if you like photography, write about how to take good pictures, review YouTube Videos on photography, Just take pictures and post as a blog item. You can write about just anything. You have to ensure that you are educating your readers. People are always searching for how to do something or make something. You can write these kinds of post or even review products and services. If your interest is in fashion, food, inspiration, or any other topic, just go ahead and write. Researching topics in your areas of interest will help you identify what to write about. Remember to make *Google Alerts* your friend.

Your topic can also be general. That is, you just write about anything and everything. You could even make your blog a personal journal that you want to share with the public. Perhaps, someone can learn something from your own personal experience. People like stories, especially personal stories. I learned about a couple who decided to home school their kids by travelling across the United States and writing about their daily experiences. The good news is that they also made money doing that. I also have a website called Bukola Inspires that I use to motivate others with my personal stories. You can check it out here http://www.bukolainpsires.com.

How do you make your blogging easy? You may ask. There is a professional blogger who has helped by creating a blogging calendar that you can adopt. You can check him out on his website, www.problogger.com. See a screen shot of a blog calendar he created to help bloggers in their blogging journey. You will notice that he used **Google Calendar**, which is also another free application on your Gmail account.

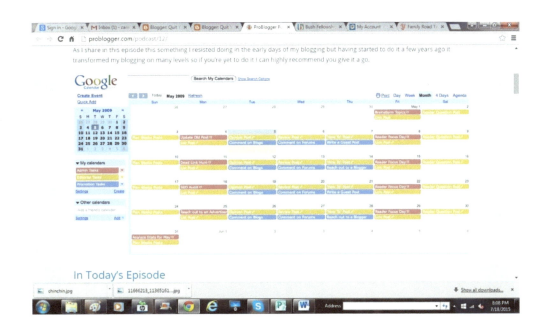

Darren Rowse, Founder of *Problogger* has a plan for writing that will make the process easier. He called it *31 Days to Build a Better Blog*. That is what he has also used to create the blogging calendar to help both old and new bloggers. He also created a Podcast on this blogging exercise. In addition, he has a Workbook titled *31 Days to Build Better Blog Workbook* for purchase. He has it on sale for $29.99 at the time of revising this book.

According to Rowse, his 31-day blogging exercise comprised of taking small actions because, "Inspiration without implementations is empty."

Set Up Social Media Pages

For you to be interested in this book, I am guessing that you are already on at least one social media platform. The most popular where people spend time whining or sharing valuable information is Facebook. I think that Facebook founders were smart by using "Friend" when they created this platform. As a result, people don't feel like they are chatting with perfect strangers when they are, because, they feel that they are interacting as friends on the platform. This same thinking has made it easier for marketers to take great advantage of the platform to generate revenue either organically or through paid advertisements.

I have benefit from Facebook through both means. I have done Facebook advertisements and I have also gained clients organically. Organic means of gaining client is when you don't pay for advertisements; rather, you just have your fan page, where a potential client finds you and pay for your products or services. Another thing with having a Facebook fan page is, when you get the right people to like your page, they can turn into paying clients.

A Facebook marketer who uses Facebook to promote his contents and also gains clients is Jon Loomer. You can check him out at www.jonloomer.com. He has great content that you can use to grow on Facebook as a content marketer. You have to see yourself as a content marketer to make money from your blogs.

Having your mind set right is pivotal to your success on social media platforms such as Facebook, otherwise, you will just continue with the millions who only consume but never sell or make money on Facebook.

Before I go any further, I will recommend starting with at least two social media platforms depending on what you are blogging about. You could make it three or four by adding video platforms. The four platforms that I will recommend you start with are Facebook, Google Plus, YouTube, and Periscope.

Facebook: If you already have a Facebook personal account. You will now go ahead and create a fan page for your blog site. To make it an easy process, click on any of the fan page that you are following on Facebook. When you do so, scroll down to look for a green box on the left corner at the bootom of items listed under the page's thumbnail picture will say *Create Page.* Click on it to start creating your fan page. See illustration below.

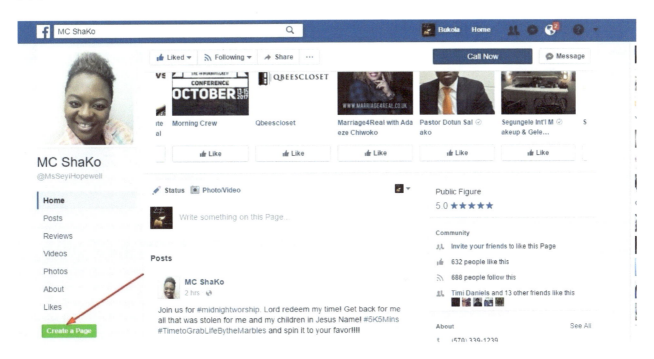

The next step is to choose what category you think that your blog post is about. Once you click Create Page the illustration below is what the next page will look like.

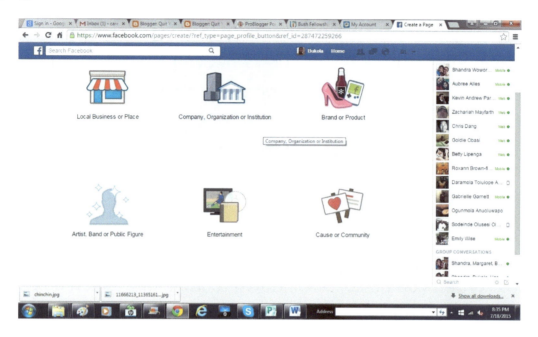

Choose the one that most fit and continue with the process until you get to the end. Check out this blog link for a step by step direction provided by *Nuts and Bolt Media* on how to set up a Fan page for your blog https://www.nutsandboltsmedia.com/how-to-create-a-facebook-fan-page-for-your-blog/.

Google Plus: Once you open a new Gmail account, you can open a *Google Plus* account because it's a Google product. Otherwise, when you set up your *Blogger* account, you can open your *Google Plus* account. When you do that, whenever you publish a "New Post" it automatically posts on *Google Plus* once you set it to automatically post on *Google Plus* in your *Blogger settings*.

YouTube: YouTube is a video sharing platform. You can make videos to post on YouTube, and then you publish it as a "New Post" on your blog site. You can get subscribers on YouTube and build an audience through that platform.

Periscope: This no longer a new application that allows you to do live broadcast. By now, live broadcast is no longer new to you. Facebook and some other social media platform followed Periscope to allow users to create live videos on their platforms. You can share what you are doing with your followers and they can comment or chat with you live. Periscope is a Twitter application. If you already have a Twitter account, while opening your account on Periscope, it can ask you to sign up using your Twitter account. Mind you, I purposely did not talk about setting up a Twitter account here. But if you want to, you can also open a Twitter account. You can create your Periscope account through this link https://www.periscope.tv/.

Google AdSense

Google AdSense is your money making machine. Wait a minute. Proceed with caution. This is not a quick money making machine. You have to put in the work to see the result. It is one thing to set up Google AdSense; it is another thing entirely to start making money from it. It took me more than a year to make my first $100 from Google AdSense. And, I know why. It was because I lacked consistency. You have to be consistent at publishing and learning more about how to place you AdSense codes to see the kinds of result you want.

In addition, you have to write the kinds of content that will make visitors click on the google adverts on your blog site. To sign up for Google AdSense is easy. It only takes three steps. You can click on this link to sign up. http://www.google.com/adsense/start/. It will take you to the screenshot below.

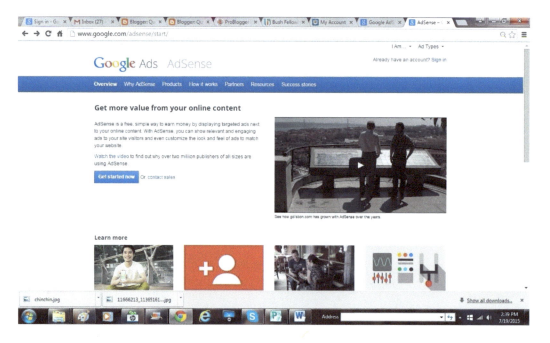

I will recommend taking the time to review all the wealth of information provided by Google on how Google AdSense works. It will help you a lot in maximizing your revenue once you get started. The cool thing about Google AdSense is that you don't have to worry about placing an expired code on your website. Google ensures that the advertisements placed on your site are relevant and current. See the screenshot below to see "How it works" page.

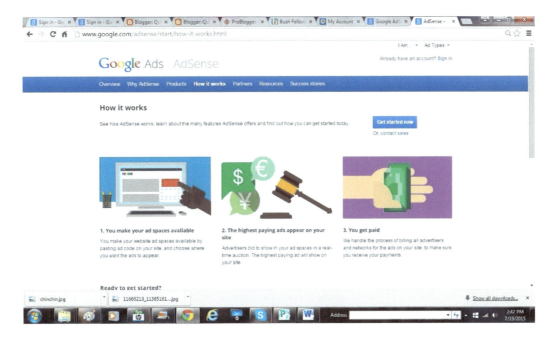

I can assure you that it can be overwhelming trying to learn a lot at the same time. It can even be worse when you don't know exactly what to focus on to start getting results. Below is a screenshot of the first set of things you need to pay attention. It is called the *Publishers Tools.* Use it to learn and understand how Google AdSense works. Check to make sure that Google Adsense is available to your country. When you apply, you will find out if you are approved or not.

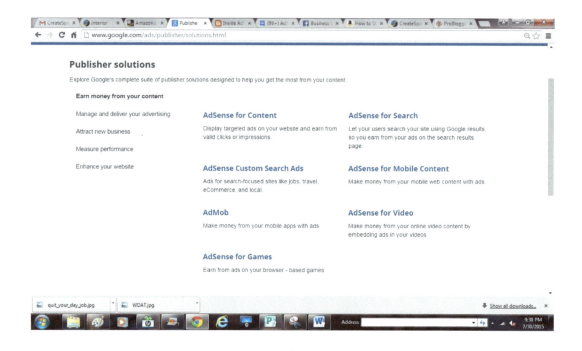

There are other avenues where you can make money from your blog. Some are called *Affiliate Marketing* (advertisers supplying you with advertisement codes to place on your site. If your site refers someone to their site who makes a purchase, you get paid certain amount that the publisher is willing to pay). You can go further by signing up to *Affiliate Marketing*.

One of the popular Affiliate Marketer is *Commission Junction*. They have their rules and policies. If you are interested, you can check *Commission Junction* out at this link http://www.cj.com/. The down side is that you have to monitor the code to make sure it is current. Otherwise, if someone clicks an expired code, you will not get paid, even if the person makes a purchase. It has happened to me before.

Google has similar product called *Google Ads Publisher*. You have to sign up. You don't automatically have the account because you have *Google AdSense*. The way *Google Ad Publisher* works is just like

Commission Junction. You are supplied with codes. It is important to note that, you have to bid for codes sometimes. Other times, an advertiser may review your site before agreeing to have advertisement placed on your site. Just like *Google AdSense* and *Commission Junction*, I will recommend that you take the time to learn about *Google Ad Publisher*. Once you understand how it works, you will not take too long to start reaping the benefits. See a screenshot of the *Google Ad Publisher* below. You can click on this link to take you to the website http://www.google.com/ads/publisher/.

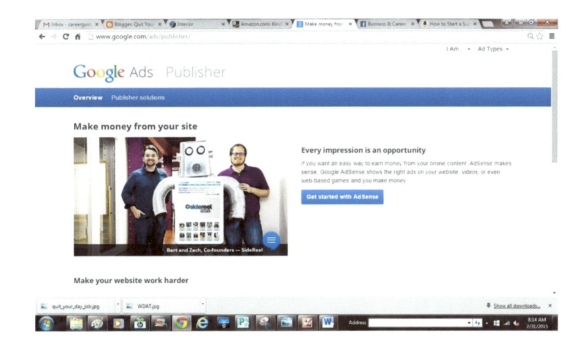

Direct Advertisement and sponsored posts: As you grow your blog site, direct marketers may reach out to you by themselves or on behalf of their client. Such was the case for me when a public relations Agency reached out to me from the United Kingdom to host a blog for their client on my hair braiding website, www.bukolabraiding.com. So, you never know where money will be coming for you. The beauty of the online is that you can make money from any part of the world without sending a physical product out.

Sometimes, the actual client will reach out soliciting for Affiliate marketing, or asking you to host a picture or prepared flier that is an advertisement on your blog site. A site I stumbled upon while trying to find software for my book cover is www.boxshot.com. They are looking for bloggers or anyone with a web presence to send clients their way through their affiliate program. They are willing to pay $60 for each referral. See the screen shot below.

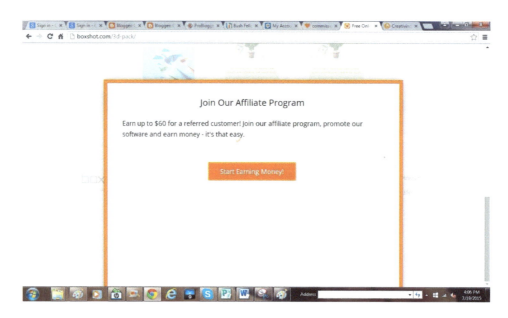

There are several other affiliate programs out there. If you are interested, just google search "Affiliate programs" and you will have various affiliate programs to choose from. Another popular one, similar to *Commission Junction* is *Click Bank* and you can click this link to get there http://www.clickbank.com/.

Proceed with Caution: make sure that your site is fully running with regular published content for at least four weeks before you start signing up for *Google Adsense*, affiliate links or reaching out to advertisers. They are going to check to see if the site is running and up to date.

Monitoring your blog site for performance

Now that you know the steps to get you started to making money blogging, it is valuable to be able to see what works and what does not. That is where the word "analytics" come in. I will recommend using *Google Analytics*. It is a free product offered by Google to help both advertisers and publishers understand how to maximize profit. In fact, Rowse recommends that you install *Google Analytics* as soon as you set up your blogger site. This means that you should set up the analytics before you even publish your first post. It will help you to track data and help you to understand what is working or not on your site. He affirms that, "Google Analytics is the most powerful stats program I've come across and best of all it's completely free."

Google Analytics: Sign up for Google Analytics to help you understand how to improve on your content, drive more traffic to your blog site, and most of all, make more money consistently on your blog site. Here is a link to Google Analytics http://www.google.com/intl/en/analytics/. See screenshot below of how to sign up for *Google Analytics*. There is the premium version, but that is for enterprises, so don't worry about the premium, just sign up and enjoy the free version. Once you sign up and get your "Google Analytics Id" head over to your blog site under "Settings", click on "Other" you will see where to add the "Google Analytics Id". Add it so that your site can be tracked. This tracking is important for advertisers and marketers who may be interested in doing sponsored posts or just buying advert space on your site.

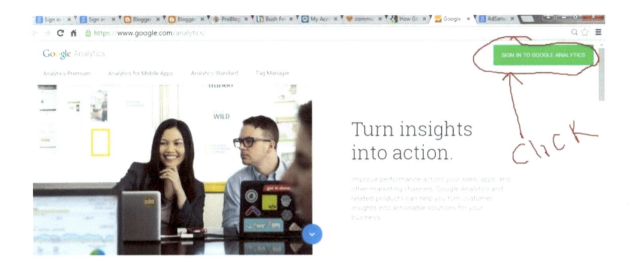

Turn insights into action.

Improve performance across your sites, apps, and other marketing channels. Google Analytics and related products can help you turn customer insights into actionable solutions for your business.

Solutions for your business.

Bonus

I have decided to add a little bonus to this revised version. The following are optional, but if you take advantage of them, they will help grow your site and following.

- Webmaster Tools
- Instagram
- MailerLite
- Canva

Webmaster Tools: This is another product that you can use to track your website. Also known as the Google Search Console, you can add your site and verify the ownership of your site on this platform. This is a link to go to webmaster tools, https://www.google.com/webmasters/tools/home. You are also able to get to the link from your blogger site backend. Click on "Add a Property" to add your website to the search console. Follow the prompts to verify your site. You can use your blogger site or *Google Analytics ID* to verify ownership of your site.

Instagram: I hope by now you know what *Instagram* is. It is a picture sharing platform, but a lot of influencers and content creators are using it to make money. Depending on how big your following is, brands could reach out to you to post for them and pay you for it. You can create text images using a platform like Canva and post your pictures on I*nstagram*. You can also do live videos or what they call *Instagram* Stories on *Instagram* to educate and also benefit.

MailerLite: This is an email marketing tool. You will need to verify your website to be able to sign up for *MailerLite*. Like I mentioned with

Google Adsense, take the first four weeks to build your site with content before applying for *MailerLite*. With it, you will be able to capture people's email that you will communicate with regularly about happenings on your website. These people are most likely to buy your digital or physical products. They can also help you spread the news. You have to be careful of selling an affiliate link or third-party products using your email list, otherwise, you could be penalized for it. In fact, your account could be suspended, so follow the rules of *MailerLite* and you will be fine.

Canva: This is a platform where you can design professionally looking pictures as a rookie designer. It's easy to use, especially if you don't have any designing skills. They have premade templates that you can choose from. You can even design the image for your blogger site header with *Canva*. I designed all my images with *Canva*. So, check it out here https://www.canva.com/.

In closing, I will like to thank you for giving me the time to give you these few nuggets that I have used, and which many bloggers are using out there to make money. I want to remind you that it is not a day's journey. It is also not a quick fix money making venture. You have to take the time to study and put effort into what you are doing to get your desired results.

If you feel overwhelmed with just these few tips, I can help you. I will help you set everything up from scratch and all you will need to start with is blogging, adding codes to your blog site, and watch your revenue grow. I would even show you how to do it yourself after setting you up.

You can contact me for questions, suggestions, and comments at info@bukolabraiding.com, lovebuky@gmail.com, and Bukola@bukolaoriola.com.

You call also connect with me via my website

www.bukolaoriola.com, blog site, http://allthingsbukolaoriola.blogspot.com/.

Get regular updates from me via social media

Twitter: @bukolaoriola

Periscope: @bukolaoriola (search for my name once you sign up)

Facebook: BukolaL.Oriola

Google Plus: Bukola Oriola

Instagram: @BukolaOriola

Facebook Closed Group: Business & Career Matters

Academy: Empowerment and Hope Academy

Good luck! Happy blogging and most of all make money.

About the Author

Bukola Oriola is a speaker, author, mentor, advocate, entrepreneur, consultant, and member, U.S. Advisory Council on Human Trafficking. Appointed by President Barack Obama in December 2015, Oriola is also an award winning journalist and a survivor of labor trafficking and domestic violence.

She depicts her experiences in a book, "Imprisoned: The Travails of a Trafficked Victim", to serve as an eye opener about human trafficking to everyone around the world. Sequel to that is her newly released book, "A Living Label: An Inspirational Memoir and Guide", where she documented her journey as a survivor and advocate to inspire other survivors. She has dedicated her life to helping others by sharing her story, and offering practical solutions to service providers, clinics, community members, and law enforcement on how to help victims of human trafficking and domestic violence.

She was highlighted as OVC Consultant Spotlight in January 2017 for Human Trafficking Awareness Month and awarded Change Maker 2009 by the Minnesota Women's Press for her courage. She also received the Empowerment Award in May 2016 from the Student Senate at Metropolitan State University, Minnesota for her inspiring work in human trafficking advocacy. Graduated in Spring 2017, She is a recipient of the President's Outstanding Student Award and was selected to give the commencement speech on behalf of graduating students on May 1, 2017 at Metropolitan State University, St. Paul, Minnesota.

Ms. Oriola is the producer of Imprisoned Show, a TV talk show dedicated to educating the public about human trafficking, reinforcing awareness, and advocating for victims of human trafficking and domestic abuse. She earned an associate's degree in Mass Communication from the Polytechnic Ibadan, Oyo, Nigeria, and received her Bachelor's of Art Degree with a focus on Community Leadership and Diversity from the Metropolitan State University, St. Paul, Minnesota in 2017. Oriola is the founder, The Enitan Story, a nonprofit organization with a mission to advocate for victims and empowers survivors of human trafficking and domestic abuse, and owner, Bukola Braiding and Beauty Supply, LLC. She is an inspiration to many and an entrepreneur who uses her knowledge to build and empower other entrepreneurs.

References & Resources

All Things Bukola Oriola: http://allthingsbukolaoriola.blogspot.com/.

Blogger: www.blogger.com

Box Shot: www.boxshot.com.

Bukola Braiding: www.bukolabraiding.com

Click Bank: http://www.clickbank.com/.

Commission Junction: http://www.cj.com/.

Facebook: www.facebook.com.

Google Adsense: http://www.google.com/adsense/start/.

Google Analytics: http://www.google.com/intl/en/analytics/.

Google Plus: www.googleplus.com

Google Publisher: http://www.google.com/ads/publisher/.

Jon Loomer: www.jonloomer.com.

Linda Ikeji's Blog: http://lindaikeji.blogspot.com/.

Nuts and Bolt Media: https://www.nutsandboltsmedia.com/how-to-create-a-facebook-fan-page-for-your-blog/

Periscope: https://www.periscope.tv/.

Problogger: www.problogger.com.

Twitter: www.twitter.com

YouTube: www.youtube.com